ART DOSSIER junior

Original title: *Il cuore della statua*
Text: Gloria Fossi
Translation: Catherine Frost
Illustrations: Matteo Vattani
Art director: Raffaele Anello

Photographs:
All illustrations belong to Archivio Giunti except Fotolia.com: © Federico Neri p. 44;
© Marie Sacha p. 45

www.giunti.it

© 2013 Giunti Editore S.p.A.
Via Bolognese 165 - 50139 Firenze - Italia
Via Borgogna 5 - 20122 Milano - Italia

First edition: June 2013

Reprint	Year
6 5 4 3 2 1 0	2016 2015 2014 2013

MISTO
Carta da fonti gestite
in maniera responsabile
FSC® C023532

Printed by Giunti Industrie Grafiche S.p.A. - Prato (Italy)

GLORIA FOSSI

The heart
of the statue

illustrations by
Matteo Vattani

A story with...

MICHELANGELO

G GIUNTI Junior

How quiet it is...
hey... is anybody there?
I don't want to spend the whole night alone!
What happened? Did you forget all about me?

I'm homesick...
I wonder if Mama, at home,
is looking at this beautiful moon!

Well, what's funny about that? I have a mama too, you know!
She is tall, big, beautiful and white all over,
and her name is Ciregiola.
Yes! It really is a mountain!
I have lots of brothers and sisters too,
but they are far away, scattered all over the world.
I wonder if they've been luckier than me!

Because as soon as we are born, when men begin to poke
and jab at Mama all over with those iron blades, to tickle her
and slice us off like pieces of cake, a little heart forms
in each block of marble. But only Mama can see it!
And knows what kind of sculpture we will become, one day,
though it's not so easy to see, since we are all lying
inside stone cocoons! Except for Mama,
it's only the artists who know we can become statues.

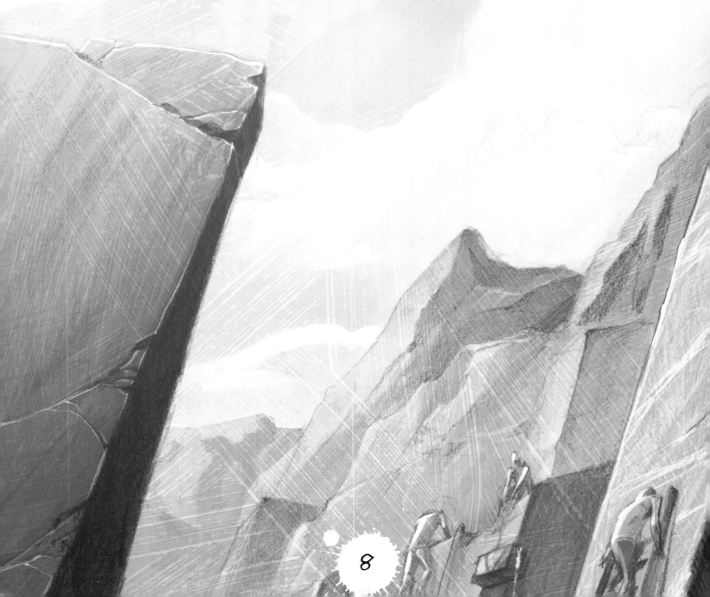

With me instead, nobody has managed to turn me into a statue.
Because I'm a very strange block of marble,
and nobody knows what to do with me.
I am long and heavy, but also very narrow.
I am enormous; colossal, in fact.

When I was born, Mama smiled at me and said,
  "You are little, but you have got a lot of courage!"
  But if I'm little, what good is all this marble?

As soon as the men saw me, they began to grumble and complain.
Then they loaded me on a very light boat,
with two triangular sails that snorted and puffed all the time because
it was so hard for them to pull the boat up the river and
they were afraid they would sink. They really made me mad!
Then we finally arrived at this city, which is called Florence.

I was a marble colossus over five metres high,
and all the Florentines, as soon as they saw me, would exclaim:
"Ooohhhhh, look at that giant!"
I was so ashamed I wanted to hide,
to dive into the river and sink underwater!
But it's not so easy for me to move around.
And so I became known to all as the "Giant".

14

And then they brought me here.
Nobody knew what to do with me.
"Too tall", some of them said.
"Too narrow", said others.
Now years have passed since they dumped me
in this storeroom behind the Cathedral.

15

Even when they built the great dome, nobody wanted
to put me up there with the other blocks of marble.
Filippo Brunelleschi, the great architect, had invented
a system for hoisting up the heaviest stones.
But I was even too big for that!

17

And so they asked a sculptor, Agostino,
to carve out of my marble a figure to stand outside the Cathedral.
Poor Agostino! It was midsummer, and really hot!
He sweated, skinned his hands, worked hard with his assistant.
And once in a while he yelled:
"Baccellino, what do you think you're doing! Don't you see
that you're chipping this poor block of marble by hitting it so hard?"
But even Agostino finally gave up. Also because Baccellino,
instead of helping him, had made a lot of mistakes.

Then they thought of another artist
considered a great genius, Leonardo da Vinci.
But he didn't even want to try.
He had other things to do, it seems.

There, remembering Mama has helped me to pass the time.
It's already morning. And it's really hot!
Of course, it's midsummer again but many, many years have passed
since poor Agostino tried to sculpt me.
If I'm not mistaken, in fact, it must be 1501 already!

But what's happening now?
Who is this strange man walking around me
and examining me from every angle?
Ha, ha! Now he's tickling me, with those big hands!
And I can see a smile in his eyes,
under that scowling face!
It's strange, but my little sleeping heart
has suddenly woken up and begun to beat again.
Now I'm smiling back at him!
Well, what's funny about that?
You think I don't know how to smile?
Of course I do!

And now a lot of people are looking at me with curiosity,
while Michelangelo, that's his name,
is studying the quality of my marble.
Maybe he wants to know if I'm strong enough
to stand the blows of his scalpel.

"That's enough, Granaccio",
he says to a friend beside him.
"All these people standing around are beginning
to get on my nerves. I can't work in peace.
Give me a hand and we'll build
a fence of wood and mortar!"

And suddenly… poof!
Let's jump ahead in time!

I feel I've been a part of Michelangelo's life
from the time he was a boy, as if we had always been together.
Because I can read his heart, just the way he reads mine!

And here we are in the year 1482. There are two friends working
in the shop of the painter Domenico Ghirlandaio.
Francesco, known as Granaccio, is a handsome young man
with such delicate features that painters often use him as a model.
He has just turned 18, and is a friend of Michelangelo.
He too is a handsome boy, only 12 years old,
and a little sad because he lost his mother a few years ago.

At this time, Ghirlandaio is working on a very
important project, in the church of Santa Maria Novella.
"Michelangelo!", Granaccio calls out.
"What are you doing with that pencil in your hand?
Mix the colours, hand us the brushes,
the bucket of water and the rags!"
"Excuse me!", the boy replies, leaving his drawing at once.

But his friend comes down from the scaffolding.
Michelangelo is like a brother to Granaccio
and he wants to protect the boy
from punishment by their master, Ghirlandaio.
"Master Domenico!!! Come and see what a beautiful drawing!!!
Michelangelo has drawn a picture of the artists at work,
up on the scaffolding in the chapel!"

Ghirlandaio comes down,
looks at the drawing and can't believe his eyes:
"But you are the best of all!
You're even better than I am!!!"

Days and months go by.
It's now a beautiful day in September.
"Come on in, boys", says Bertoldo,
the sculptor of the garden
of Lorenzo the Magnificent.
"I know you both, you are Granaccio,
and you are the son of Lodovico Buonarroti.

I saw you the other day
in Ghirlandaio's workshop.
He told me you're the best of all!
I'd be happy to have you come work
with me in the garden."

"But I don't want to be a gardener !"
cries the young Michelangelo.
"And who said you would be?
Come here, boy. Don't you see that this garden is full of statues?
Look at that fountain, with a dolphin carved on it."
"It's splendid!"

"And this marble bust. It was made by an ancient Roman sculptor, centuries ago. The Magnificent has put all his finest sculptures here in this garden."

"Granaccio! Look at this head, how beautiful it is!", says Michelangelo.
"It's the head of a faun", Bertoldo explains. "A being that lives
in the woods, and has pointed ears and the feet of a goat."
"Can I copy it?"
"Of course, come back whenever you like."

A few days later, Michelangelo has finished his sculpture:
"Granaccio, come and see, I have finished the faun! I gave him
a laughing mouth. How do you like it?"
"I'm not Granaccio, but I'll look at it anyway", says the voice
of the Magnificent Lorenzo, who comes to the garden every day.
"Excellent! But you have carved an old faun and left him all his teeth!
Don't you know that some of them are always missing at his age?"

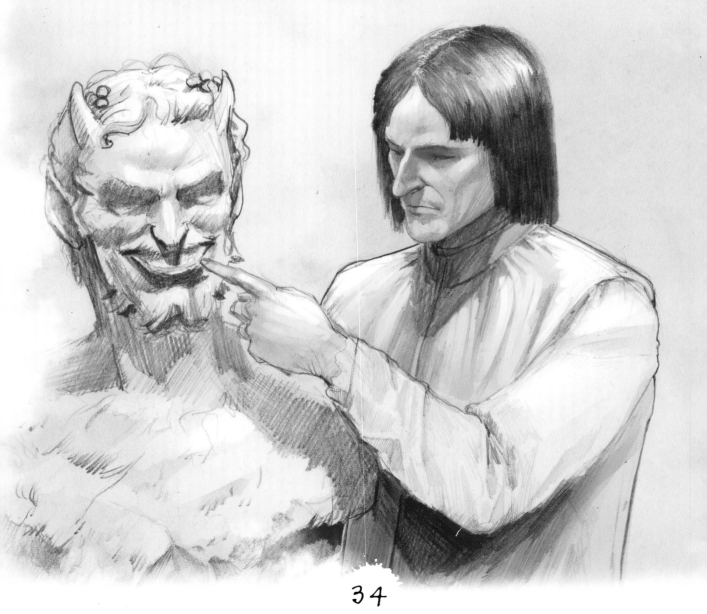

"Hmmm... I hate to say it, but he's right",
thinks Michelangelo, who can't wait for Lorenzo to go
so he can correct the error. And he removes a pair of teeth
from the faun's upper jaw. The next day Lorenzo comes back.
"You make me laugh Michelangelo, but I'm laughing with joy.
You are really good! Tomorrow I want to speak to your father
and ask him to let you come live at my house,
where you'll find everything you need to work."

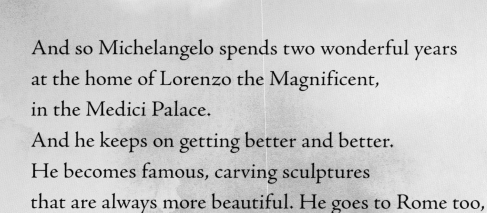

And so Michelangelo spends two wonderful years
at the home of Lorenzo the Magnificent,
in the Medici Palace.
And he keeps on getting better and better.
He becomes famous, carving sculptures
that are always more beautiful. He goes to Rome too,
where he studies the works of the ancient Romans,
and even begins to write poetry.
Many years later, in Rome, he would design
the most beautiful dome in the world!

In Florence, Michelangelo often goes
with Granaccio to meet their friends
in Piazza San Giovanni,
near Giotto's Bell Tower.

"Listen, Granaccio, I have an idea.
Do you remember that giant block of marble
that the Cathedral workers keep
in that big room in the storage deposit?"
"Of course I remember it,
not even Messer Leonardo wanted to sculpt it."
"I know, but I can do it.
Leonardo is old, he's a genius
but he never finishes anything.
I know I can do it!"

"You're out of your mind!"
"If that's what you think,
then I'll tell you a secret. I'm going to start tomorrow.
The Gonfaloniere, the head of the Florentine Republic,
has just officially asked me to.

And poof! Here we are back in 1501!

A few days after the midsummer holidays,
Michelangelo has begun to sculpt me.
And the funny thing is that the deeper
he carves with his scalpel, the lighter I feel!
Now I know what Mama meant
when she said I was little, but I had a lot of courage.
In my marble cocoon, Michelangelo
recognised the statue of a boy
who once challenged the giant Goliath to fight,
and killed him with a slingshot.
His name was David, and he was certainly not
as tall as a giant. But he was a giant
in courage and intelligence, and that was
how he managed to defeat a terrible enemy,
much stronger than he was.

I can't wait to get out of here, finally in my new form.
Michelangelo has freed me at last.
It's really true, obstacles don't exist, when your heart is big!

43

It's all true!

This story is all true! Well, except for the fact that the block of marble is speaking... Even today, in those mountains, the **Alpi Apuane**, they still mine the white marble of Carrara, unique of its kind and very beautiful. And a great many artists go there from all over the world to carve sculptures. The marble is also used in many countries to make floors, furniture, columns and numerous other things.

And then, Michelangelo was really a child prodigy. He was born in **1475** at Caprese, a town near Arezzo. He lost his mother at an early age, and his father sent him to work in Ghirlandaio's shop while still very young. He learned the trade immediately and remained a life-long friend of the painter **Francesco Granacci** (known as Granaccio), the boy he met there. Michelangelo was always restless. He was very reserved and created

The Apuane Alps

a great many of his works all by himself, without asking help from anyone, like the other artists did. And he lived a very long time, to the age of 89.

In addition to the **David**, he sculpted many other works, including the **Slaves**, who really look like captives trying to free themselves from the marble. Some of them can be seen along with the David at the **Galleria dell'Accademia in Florence**.

But Michelangelo was not just a great sculptor. He wrote intense poetry, and above all he was a superb painter. In Rome, for the pope, he created an unrivalled masterpiece: the great frescoes in the **Sistine Chapel**. No one else has ever managed alone to create such exceptional works!

44

Experiments

How would you like to make a sculpture yourself?

First of all, prepare the modelling material, but get an adult to help you, and try not to dirty up your room! You can choose between:

Salt dough

Ingredients:

- a cup of flour (cake flour, if possible)
- a cup of salt
- a cup of water at room temperature

Mix all the ingredients together and knead them into a soft, re-sistant dough (you can add a teaspoon of seed oil and a teaspoon of vinavyl if you want to). Put the salt dough in a plastic bag and store it in a cool place, if possible in the refrigerator, to keep it from drying too quickly.

Rice dough

Ingredients:

- 1 heaping tablespoon of seed oil
- 1 teaspoon of lemon juice
- rice starch, 300 g
- a plastic bag
- 300 gr. of vinyl

With a spatula, mix all the ingredients together. Place the dough on a waterproof ta-blecloth, or on a marble counter. To model it more easily, dust your hands with starch. Work the dough well to form a soft, smooth mixture. Cover it with transparent film and let it rest for 24 ore.

And now, let your creativity loose! When you have finished your sculpture, take a pic-ture of it and glue it onto the last page in this book. Your work of art will be framed!!

Quiz

Here's a quiz to answer with your friends and family!

1) What do you call the material Michelangelo used to sculpt the David??

A Pietra serena
B Plasteline
C Marble
D Terra cotta

2) Who was Lorenzo the Magnificent?

A The Lord of Mantua
B A Florentine sculptor
C A Roman cardinal
D The Lord of Florence

3) What were Ghirlandaio's pupils making?

A Pots and pans
B Tables and chairs
C Drawings, paintings and frescoes

4) Was Michelangelo a sculptor only?

A Yes
B No, he was a also a painter and a poet

5) What other work is he famous for?

A The Mona Lisa
B The frescoes in the Sistine Chapel
C A bronze David

ANSWERS: C, D, C, B, B.

46

An artist like Michelangelo

Glue the photo of your sculpture here! And fill in the plate under the frame with the name of the artist (yourself!) and the title of the work, just like in the museums!

De Chirico

Giotto

Modigliani

Matisse

Monet

Picasso

Raffaello

Vermeer

Klimt

Michelangelo

Leonardo

Van Gogh

Warhol

Caravaggio

Tiziano

Kandinskij

Rembrandt

Botticelli

Dalì

Magritte

ART DOSSIER junior

Ask your bookshop for
"The secret notebook"
a story with LEONARDO